THE NEW SUPERPOWER

by
James Hilgendorf

Library of Congress Control Number: 2007926464

ISBN: 978-1-929159-19-6

Published by The Tribute Series, P.O. Box 12144,
Eugene, OR. 97440, (800) 898-9441

CONTENTS

THE NEW SUPERPOWER

PROLOGUE

For all of us who were not there, or who were not even born at that time, here is what happened:

At 8:15 a.m., August 6th, 1945, the first atomic bomb used on a city detonated over Hiroshima, Japan.

In the first fraction of a millionth of a second, the temperature at the core of this exploding universe reached millions of degrees centigrade - 10,000 times hotter than the sun's surface. Surreal blinding light expanded across the sky and the city, instantly vaporizing, burning and charring beyond recognition thousands of human beings. Within a kilometer of the epicenter, peoples' hearts and livers and kidneys and eyes and brains disintegrated in a fraction of a second. One man,resting on some steps, disappeared immediately, leaving only a shadow scorched into the stone.

Almost simultaneously came an enormous shockwave, traveling at the speed of sound, smashing and grinding and pulverizing everything in sight. Raging, wind-whipped firestorms broke out all over the city.

In a seeming moment, the city of Hiroshima had ceased to exist. The center of the city was levelled and more than 60,000 buildiings were destroyed.

Survivors describe scenes of utter horror:

> "I looked around me, then gasped. The scenes before me were not of this Earth. They could be called a living hell. Shattered heads. A dazed mother covered with blood, still clutching her dead baby. A child with skin peeling from his entire body, shrieking from inside a collapsed building. Internal organs spilling out of bodies. Lines of completely naked people. Images of inconceivable carnage burned themselves into my mind, and every time I recall them, the tears begin flowing before I realize it."

Another:

> "It was exactly like a procession of ghosts. I saw one man with hundreds of glass shards piercing his body from the waist up. The skin of another man had peeled off his entire upper body, exposing a mass of red flesh. A woman was covered in blood, one eyeball grotesquely hanging out of its socket. Next to a mother whose skin had completely peeled off lay a loudly crying baby, its body an unprotected mass of red flesh. A number of corpses lay scattered about. A dead woman's internal organs had burst out onto the ground around her. It was utterly gruesome, a living hell indescribable in words."

These words of survivors are shocking. They are meant to be shocking. They are an attempt to convey a new, and heretofore unimagined, reality.

If there was ever any question of mens' and womens' power over events, it was seemingly annihilated once and for all in the summer of 1945, at Hiroshima, and then once again, a few days later, at Nagasaki.

What happened that summer was so overwhelming, so incomprehensible in its devastation and implications, that the psyche of people everywhere folded inward. There was an enormous implosion of collective belief in the future itself. It was something that could not be faced directly. The truth of what happened had to be buried deeply. This is still our reality.

At its deepest level, what the bomb instilled into the human psyche was a deep and all-pervading sense of powerlessness.

We subsumed our own lives to the power of the bomb. We embraced the bomb itself. With this bomb, we became the world's greatest superpower; and from that moment, we have continued to design and build and point new megadeath weapons at all four corners of the globe that are thousands of times more destructive than the bombs that wiped Hiroshima and Nagasaki off the map.

With these bombs we literally now hold within our hands the power to completely destroy life on this planet Earth.

How to function within this reality?

What of the individual?

Amid the horrors of the past century, the hundreds of millions slaughtered and the spectre of thousands of bombs thousands of more times deadly pointed this very moment at you and I,who is it that can argue that any man or woman or child on the face of this planet matters?

This book is about that reality.

It is also about other realities: What is the nature of our universe? Who are we? What is life and death? What can one person do?

It is about the buried dream of America.

It is about a new power emerging, more dazzling and potent than ten thousand suns breakiing over the rivers of Hiroshima.

This power issues forth from the core and heart of the universe itself, and reveals itself only through the heart of one man or woman: then fuses with the hearts of myriads of other men and women, finally hemhorraging forth in a chain reaction of blinding white nuclear force.

It is justice. It is hope. It is compassion.

It is you and I together.

It is the new superpower.

THE BURIED DREAM OF AMERICA

The following are recent random samplings of student responses to the question:

"How do you feel about your future, and the future of your country?

>"I'm almost afraid to bring my children into this world. I don't want them to deal with some of the things they may have to deal with. If we ever go to world war, it's over. I think everybody's walking on eggshells, especially us, even though we portray this big, strong, magnificent country that wants to control everything and help everybody, we're really only hurting ourselves, because there are so many problems here. And everybody else sees it, I feel, but us. We have our own problems and issues that we need to concentrate on more, instead of trying to make the world a better place. It's not going to help sending any more troops over

there to tell people what they want. I think we ought to concentrate on ourselves first."

".....Tom Brokaw wrote this book - America's Greatest Generation - and I think that's what happened. People don't love America like they used to. Maybe we need to change the dynamics on the ground. I mean give people healthcare, invest in people and show some affection. It goes a long ways."

"....I"m just worried that greed has such an overwhelming impact on our government and how things are run. We're heavily impacted by money, and that's how things are run. I'm concerned with politics, I think it's a pretty ugly system. I just wonder how long it will be until there's some sort of breakdown, and what that's going to look like, because I don't think we can continue exploiting and running things the way we are right now."

"....I don't feel like I have a whole lot of power in the situation right now. I feel pretty small when I think about all the problems that the world is having right now."

This is the state of mind of many young people today - a feeling of disempowerment and apathy - and it is the state of mind of many others in this country of ours also, this United States of America.

Wars and devastation are wracking the world, and there seems no anchor. We entered this century hopeful that perhaps a new age was about to dawn. The terrible wars of the last century were over, the Cold War was finished, things seemed to be moving in a new direction. But in just a few short years, these dreams have been shattered.

Here are some other things young Americans had to say:

Female student:

> "....I'm uncomfortable with our presence over-seas. I'm a little bit ashamed to be an American. I feel that we've made mistakes recently. I don't really know where we're headed. It's a little scary."

Male student:

> "....I feel embarrassed a lot of the time about how we're perceived by other countries. And rightfully so. I think people are beginning to see that our standing in the world is starting to degrade pretty precipitously right now. There's a growing sense of division between Americans and other countries."

Female student:

> "....I like the ideals we've had in the past, but I think they've been bastardized by our overem-phasis on capitalism and on controlling the rest of the world. And I think in a lot of ways that this exploitative nature is what is rewarded nowadays, rather than being a good person and showing real human values, such as hon-esty, integrity, fairness, thinking about other peoples, not just looking out for yourself alone."

Male student:

"....Our priorities are perverse and shameful."

Where, in all of this, lies the dream of America? - that great dream of the future held by all people from the very beginnings of this country's founding?

What, even, is this dream?

It is a dream that has always gone beyond more mundane affairs. Yes, it was a place to start over, a place to pull your-self up by the bootstraps and make a good living or even get rich. To many, this was what America meant. People still strive for that type of dream.

But this was not then, nor now, nor ever will be, the real dream and promise of America. It was something much more intan-gible. It was a hunger and a dim hope kept alive in the hearts of all since the beginning of time. It was a cry heard down the ages from innumerable unsung men and women, voices like a swelling river gathering towards something greater, a greater life, hungry for justice, hungry for a larger, more meaningful place in the cosmos itself.

Our greatest poet, Walt Whitman, spoke of it, sensed it, knew of it in his blood and bones, and put it, as best he could, into words. Looking to the future, to the promise of America, he wrote:

> "There will soon be no more priests. Their work
> is done. They may wait awhile...perhaps a gen-
> eration or two...dropping off by degrees. A
> superior breed shall take their place...the gangs

8

of kosmos and prophets en masse shall take their place. A new order shall arise and they shall be the priests of man, and every man shall be his own priest. The churches built under their umbrage shall be the churches of men and women. Through the divinity of themselves shall the kosmos and the new breed of poets be interpreters of men and women and of all events and things. They shall find their inspiration in real objects today, symptoms of the past and future...They shall not deign to defend immortality or God or the perfection of things or liberty or the exquisite beauty and reality of the soul. They shall arise in America and be responded to from the remainder of the Earth."

This was a point in time filled not only with his voice, but with the voices of others who sensed the same imminent potential of these United States of America. There was Emerson, and Thoreau, and others.

There was something gathering, an apex of opportunities. It was democracy, real democracy, not just a sham of ballot stuffing; but the development of a new race of men and women wedded to a new myth of space and time that connected life in these States to the heartbeat of the universe itself.

Again, Whitman:

"Come, I will make the continent indissoluble,
I will make the most splendid race the sun ever shone upon...

The great poet himself perceived quite well the lapse between dream and reality. He recognized greed, stupidity, corruption, dissolution, betrayal all around him. Still he held to the dream.

Looking back, he could see, over and over, the dream die and expire in the dust of countless centuries, countless millenia; and yet, now, for the first time in history the world seemed to be converging on a new era, a nation was emerging that drew its sustenance from the worlds' peoples, black and white and brown and yellow, from an infinite variety of pasts and cultures, all converging on this magnetic land, breaking loose frrom mankind's past, new soil, a place to make dreams grow and happen, a new chapter, a new epic, in mankind's history.

It was a spiritual ground breaking.

It was a leveling of all governments, all castes, all society, all distinctions. Not the distinctions that are everywhere and have always been everywhere, the gradations of intellect, of physical strength, of wealth, of innate and inborn capacities - no, this was a new leveling, a stripping away of all of these spurious distinctions and differences, and getting down to the most fundamental of all realities - the universal human being.

This was what was promised. This is what Whitman sensed and felt in his bones, and understood with his whole being. This was the new world, the America, beckoning from the stars, a promise, after millenia, even after trillions of years, that, yes, the universe was finally coming to fruition in the heart and mind and soul of the average man and woman.

So, still, what is this dream of America?

It was, and is, to be discovered, as Whitman knew, in a new spiritual dimension.

It is what we are still struggling towards, what we are still fashioning from the deepest darkness, the corruption, the wars, the bitter feuding and division, the collapse of all civilizational structures and modes and ideas.

Everything has come to a blind alley. It has come to utter confrontations, of East and West, of Christian and Muslim and Jew, of divisional, useless politics, and the rise of terror in the hearts of men and women worldwide.

We have fashioned a physical New World, pushed and shoved and flexed our muscles from one seashore to another, built mega-cities and populated the continent with races and cultures from around the world; but the new spiritual continent has yet to take shape.

Is this dream of America even possible?

Or are we merely dreaming?

THE BUILDING OF THE BOMB

There were many men who built the bomb - the bomb that destroyed not only Hiroshima and Nagasaki, but the invisible structure and underpinnings of Western civillization. The support columns are still crumbling.

How assuring the world once looked!

A few centuries back, Newtonian physics dominated the known and unknown universe, subject to unchanging laws. There was nothing that was not subject to the eventual yoke of man's reason.

Everything seemed clear cut. There was man, the spiritual being, at the center; but beyond our blood and skin and bones and mind lay a vast outer world of fields and animals and oceans and moon, sun and stars.

It was a world completely separate from us. Our probing reason extracted from this world the secret mathematics of its

operation, and we placed a yoke upon the universe to make it serve our ends.

From Newton's time on, we believed that eventually we would unearth all the secret laws of this external universe, and infinite power would be ours. We would be masters of the cosmos.

In the last century, though, things began to unravel.

Our world above ground, in the sunlight, seemed unfazed, seemed to roll on as usual. But down below, we began to discover an extraordinary and strange world, a world of atoms and electrons and quarks and other phantom-like entities, behaving in ways utterly contradictory to reason and common sense.

We found the world 'out there' was really not 'out there'. Everything was linked somehow.

We found, for instance, that when we tried to measure the properties of electrons, the results changed simply because we were involved in doing the measuring. Because we were part of the measuring process, the outcomes changed.

We - the objective onlooker -were part of the equation.

One of the great physicists of the last century, John Wheeler, wrote:

> "Nothiing is more important about the quantum principle than this, that it destroys the concept of the world as 'sitting out there'....To describe what has happened, one has to cross out the old word 'observer' and put in its place the new word 'participator'.

16

"In some strange sense the universe is a participatory universe."

Along came other men - Heisenberg, Bohr, Einstein - men who laid the foundations for the Bomb - all wrestling with the same dilemma.

They created incredible formulas and theories which gave us lasers and neutron bombs and space stations; but never once did they truly penetrate the deeper mystery at all: What is this world out there?

We live in a world of mirrors. What we see outside mirrors ourselves. We have not yet come to this realization, though; and so we battle our reflections, tilting here, tilting there, trying to set things straight, trying to achieve mastery, bombing and destroying people if necessary, tearing up the environment, sealing ourselves off from an intractable world.

There is no way out of such a madhouse.

Who are we?

The scientists who laid the foundations and constructed the Bomb, did not know. They did not have a clue.

But from their castles of reason and logic, they constructed a device for delivering immense power, light and energy, a destructive force beyond all imagining.

And we dropped this device over Hiroshima one day to quell the horror of murder and destruction that was crashing like a dark tide over the world.

And the mirrors of the universe reflected back, in blinding white light, ourselves utterly decimating and destroying our own heart.

COURAGE

I know a young woman who encountered mental illness when she was in her early twenties, and for the next fifteen years, and even today, has struggled to overcome the effects of her illness. She works at a simple job, assembling eyeglass frames. Even with her sincere effort, she has trouble keeping up with her quota for production. She makes little money.

She lives by herself in a small one-bedroom apartment, on a busy street. It's a lonely life, and she drinks often to counter the feelings of loneliness.

About a year ago, she met a woman, about her age, who has equally daunting disabilities. This other woman suffers frequently occurring attacks of pneumonia, and has been hospitalized four times this past year. She has been at death's door a few times. She also is very prone to broken bones from the medication she is forced to take. This woman's mother lives with her, and is in her eighties, and suffers from a regressive case of Alzheimers disease. The daughter is forced to care for the mother, as well as herself. Because of their disabilities, they have heavy financial problems, and are in danger of losing their trailer home..

These two young ladies met recently, and became, within a very short time, the best of friends. They spend time together, they talk, they find they can open up to one another. They try their best to help and encourage each other. They depend on no one, only their own efforts.

Their devotion to one another is truly humbling.

During the past month, the one woman came down again with pneumonia, and was hospitalized. Her friend spent all of her available hours at her bedside, talkiing to her, encouraging her, reading to her.

They have only each other. Their lives are tenuous, and trouble-filled.

Their daily struggles are beyond most peoples' comprehension. Their sincerity and courage in battling their afflictions is beyond most peoples' comprehension. The sincerity of their friendship is beyond most peoples' comprehension.

The reason I briefly tell their story is that these are two women we should all be honoring. These are people we should direct our attention to. They are beyond you and me.

These are the ordinary men and women of America, who are extraordinary beyond anything that our puffed-up politicians, our movie stars and starlets with their millions, our financial moguls, could possibly emulate.

Until you and I and this government we call a government recognize and bend our will and resources to aid these ordinary men and women, these extraordinary ordinary men and women, you and I and this government we call a government do not deserve seats in the house of humanity.

MEETING THE BUDDHA

I met the Buddha on the street when I was thirty-three.

She was about twenty-five, driving an older car, and she pulled up to the curb, leaned out and asked me: "Do you want to go to a Buddhist meeting?"

I said no. But she handed me a card with the address of a house a few blocks away, and told me to drop by if I changed my mind.

After she drove away, I decided I would go.

There were about sixty people in the living room of the house chanting Nam Myoho Renge Kyo. I sat down and listened and watched for about five minutes, then got up and left.

The same girl came out and tried to get me to come back in. I told her I wanted nothing to do with any of it; but she would not let go. After about five minutes, I relented, mainly because there were about sixty pair of shoes on the porch, and I could not find my own. The fact of the missing shoes I credit with my introduction to the amazing Buddhism of the SGI, or Soka Gakkai International.

As the days and weeks passed, I chanted those words, Nam Myoho Renge Kyo, and I felt things change. I had had asthma all my life, and during the first few months of chanting, my asthma fazed out, never to return again. I felt more energy, my life took on a more dynamic rythym. I did not know it then, but I had entered onto an extraordinary path in life - a path of happiness that put my own life in synch with the very path of the cosmos itself.

Buddhism allowed me to see life - and my own individual life - in a clear light.

It was as though a bright mirror were held up to my eyes: and for the first time I was able to see myself - not just the physical characteristics, the lips and nose and eyes and hair, but the internal workings of happiness and unhappiness deep within my life.

I learned about karma, cause and effect, the interconnectedness of all things, the eternity of life.

I not only began to perceive how my life operated, but I also gained the power to change the patterns that kept forcing me into deadlocks and unhappiness.

This is just one example.

I had begun working in industrial real estate sales. I was fortunate to be training with a real master in the business, who taught me a great deal in a short period of time. I was making sales and leases and coming along well.

Suddenly, I made contact with a business owner who owned ten acres of prime industrial real estate in Los Angeles. This owner wanted to sell. It seemed like a great stroke of luck, since this type and size of parcel was very sought after and hard to find at that time.

My boss, who had been in the business for three decades, knew immediately of another business owner nearby who was looking to expand his business and build a large new distribution plant.

We put the buyer and seller together, and immediately drew up a contract. The commission was $100,000 - large even for those days.

Things proceeded fairly smoothly. The time for the closing of escrow was only about two weeks away.

Only one thing remained to be cleared up. The buyer wanted to build a large new building, and he wanted a soil test done on the property. So a large drilling machine was brought in, and they began to drill.

The huge drill broke on the first attempt. Second and third attempts ended with the same result, and the drilling was called off.

Some research was done on the property, and it was finally discovered that about fifty years before there had been a steel mill operating near the property, and the dross of the hot steel had been poured into a deep excavation on this property to a depth of about thirty feet.

These ten acres were one big hunk of solid steel!

The real estate deal immediately fell out of escrow and died.

I was left hanging. I needed money, and had actually already spent money for other things, confident that I would close this deal.

This episode was not just a one-time type of occurrence. I experienced this same scenario, in one way or another, many times. I would get into a new job, approach it enthusiastically, do well at the beginning, and then somewhere along the line I would hit a wall and no matter what I did there would be no results forthcoming, and the bottom would fall out. Then I would leave and go on to a new situation, only to repeat the same cycle once again.

At the end of this experience in industrial real estate, I went to talk with someone I knew who had been practicing Buddhism for a long time. I relayed the whole story.

When I finished, he asked: "What's the earliest memory you have of your childhood?"

I was taken back for a moment; then remembered very clearly an incident that happened when I was just a young infant.

My mother was with me, and I was laying in a playpen on the grass. Then she left to go up to the apartment where we lived on the second floor of a house. She was gone awhile, and I started to cry. She heard me from the apartment, but (she told me much later) she thought to herself: "He has to learn to be by himself sometime." So she let me be.

I continued to cry, then began screaming, louder and louder, for what seemed a very long time. Finally, my mother appeared and took me in her arms; but by then I was shaking uncontrollably and out of my senses.

The person whom I had come to talk to then said:

"This is the karma that's embedded deep in your life. It seems like things are happening outside yourself, in an environment that's separate from yourself, but it's all actually being generated from within your own life.

"You keep experiencing the same thing in your work, like this latest episode in real estate. Everything goes well at first, but then - at the crucial moment - you're abandoned. There's no support. You experience abandonment by the universe around you.

"This is the karma that is buried deep in your life, and keeps playing out in the circumstances of your life, and you're not even aware of it. It seems as though it's some kind of ill luck or twist of fate in your environment, but actually it's your own life projecting itself upon your universe.

"The world around us is our mirror."

And how do we change the reflection in the mirror? We have to change ourselves.

From that moment on, I began chanting those words - Nam Myoho Renge Kyo - more earnestly, to work its medicine deep into my life; and from that moment, things began to slowly, but perceptively, change.

Buddhism gave me not only an extraordinary mirror to see myself, but also the power to fundamentally alter my life for the better.

And I began changing the karma that had held me so long in its grip.

Now I feel so supported in every area of my life.

Each day I gaze into this mirror to discover more and more of who I really am.. I look into my life to discover my identity and power.

Through Buddhism, I learned that my own, and the worlds' ills cannot be cured by acting on them solely from without. We have to also find the answers within.

WHAT DO YOU THINK?

God shines forth from the faces of children.

--Would you nuke God?

SURVIVOR

Michiko Yamaoka, is a survivor of Hiroshima. She was a young girl when the bomb went off.

She later endured twenty-seven operations on her face to correct the terrible burns caused by the bomb.

> "I never expected it, looking up at the sky - the beautiful splash of light; and at the same time my face was swelling, and I thought: 'I'm going to die.' But if I died, I couldn't see my mother again, and I started walking toward ground zero.

> "To myself I said goodbye to my mother, and then the wind blew me away.

> "I found myself buried under rocks from my stomach to my head, and I heard people crying, crying for help, but no help came.

> "I heard my mother calling my name - Michiko, Michiko.

"It was my mother who found me amidst the brutality of war.

"When she pulled me out, I saw hell all around me. This one bomb changed our whole life. It was like being in hell while still alive.

"Now Hiroshima is beautiful. Children cannot believe the bomb was dropped here. The city is beautiful, but we still have victims - hibakusha - and I want to tell people the truth of what happened.

"Now I teach people the truth so that we may never have war again. I want to continue this until I die.

"I want people to know the word peace and how beautiful life is. It's always the children who get hurt in war. I don't want children to be the victims of war anymore. So until I die, I will do my best."

THE END OF TIME

It is the end of time.

The prophets were right. Fires break out, the earth bakes and shrivels, madness reigns in the heavens and oceans. There is no place to hide.

Armies position themselves on the plains. The final battle is come. A scream arises from within the collective self, oh let annihilation rain down from the heavens, we have had enough, the dream has died too many deaths, give over, hang on to anything flying in the wind. The trees uproot. The earth splits, and humanity disappears into vast crevices, down deep divides.

Save yourself. It is the end.

THE BEGINNING OF TIME

It is the beginning of time.

The prophets were wrong. Out of madness, the pure individual self emerges once again, fresh, reflecting brilliant new light.

A new kingdom is born. We are so happy, at last we arrive. The earth revives, water rushes in shining new rivulets, everything is clean and new. Plants and trees bow in deep appreciation.

Unlimited vistas appear beyond mountain crests. Now is the time to build the new civilization, riveted upon the rock of the earth, bolted down to flowers and farms and animals and birds and the moon and sun. Let it all issue forth, from the heart of here and now, forever.

Praise yourself. It is the beginning.

MY FATHER

My father worked in a factory most of his life, on a drill press punching out metal fabrications, six in the morning till three each afternoon.

He rose early, brewed himself some coffee and read the paper while everyone else in the family was sleeping. He donned an old jacket, and a bent hat, and walked alone through the early morning hours down an old road to the factory where he worked.

He came home tired, lay on the couch, napping, then ate a simple dinner, and spent the rest of the evening on the couch reading a book or, later, watching television.

His children grew up provided for, never really guessing or feeling the enormous loss he felt at tying himself to a machine day after day, with diminishing hope for himself, all his hope now in his children, his dream for himself set aside and gone and now in its place a dream for his children.

He died at a relatively early age, his dreams gone, his hopes vanished.

But his dreams, nevertheless, lived on, and still live on, in his children; took root and slowly grew and developed into flowers; and the gratitude of his children returns to the roots of his efforts and nourishes his own life prolifically; and somewhere, somehow, he knows, and is looking on enormously gladdened, joyous.

The universe is fundamentally built that way, nothing is ever lost, there is only the heart that perseveres and perseveres and perseveres.

This is the life of the Buddha. One awakened feels this in his or her heart, there is no equivocation, no doubt whatsoever.

The Buddha is the very life of the universe itself.

As one gazes into the mirror, one sees one's father and mother and all of the numberless beings coming and going, all the anger and hatreds, loves and joys, and it is one's own life. One sees in the mirror everything, and praises and appreciates all. Everything is forcing one to grow, to develop and expand the heart, to embrace all of creation.

Who is this person, who, in his unparalleled mercy, took me into his family, and scripted a story of failure and death, and vented his frustration and anger at his sons and wife, and scolded and criticized them all, and fought and displayed his demons openly, and died that one day still working and tied to that heartless machine manufacturing banal, humdrum, spiritless products for sale in a vapid America - who was this person? He was my father...but where did he come from? How could he have given me anything more?

And as I came to love the Buddha, the Buddha that is within

38

us all, this life of overwhelmiing wisdom and compassion, I came to know who my father was.

He is the Buddha himself, a being of overwhelming compassion nurturing my own life, nurturing every life, nurturing the universe itself.

He is myself, he is everyone, we are always there together.

Hand in hand, smiling, forever.

How happy my father must be!

WAR

The Bomb detonates deep within the caverns of my life and mind.

Rage, anger, an implosion of dark light. The universe around transforms and morphs into the same deadly darkness, enveloping the sun.

This is my world too. This is the world of all of us. The Bomb, the devastation could not exist and come into being if it did not exist within the deepest core of our own being.

We can destroy it all. This is our power. This is the megaton-nage of our hatreds and greed. It is utter devastation.

The war is within. This is where the battle will be lost or won.

I have to defeat the Bomb.

It's up to me. I have to win or lose.

OUR NATION TODAY

Nuclear weapons are produced for one reason: as a means of destroying mass numbers of human beings. They are killing machines par excellence. Their intent is utterly evil. And yet we, this great Christian nation, stockpile thousands of these weapons. What does this say about us as a people? How can one possibly subscribe to the basic tenets of Christianity, and still condone the possession of, and intent to use, these horrible weapons?

There can be no justification whatsoever.

CAN ONE PERSON MAKE A DIFFERENCE?

(By a female college student)

"Oh, absolutely.

"One person can totally change it, because it's a mindset, it's setting an example. It's connecting with other people, really connecting, and causing a chain reaction.

"Like, in one of the cafes on campus, there's a little sign that says: 'I'm a traveling smile, pass me on.' And it's a trivial example, but at the same time it really shows how one action can spread out among people. And if we just smiled, instead of getting in our own heads, if we just connected with other people on the street. That sets a standard that creates a social consciousness, that ripples out as well.

"And it's not like I can do something right now and feel the effect immediately. We have to get rid of all that idea of immediate gratification. We have to think that what we do today sets the foundations for greater and bigger things in the future. And that future could be the next generation, it could be four generations from now. The fact is we're planting seeds right now in Iraq that we and our grandchildren are going to feel, and I don't think we're thinking about that, and I think that individually we need to bring that into our daily discourse.

"So, yes, definitely one person can make a difference."

TODA

His name was Josei Toda.

He was the second president of the SGI, or Soka Gakkai International, the international Buddhist organization of which I am a member.

During the second world war, he and the SGI's first president, Tsunesaburo Makiguchi, were imprisoned in Japan for their uncompromising stance against militarism and the war.

Makiguchi died in prison. Toda was released, his health broken, at the end of the war.

Toda died in 1958, but seven months before his death, he gave a speech to several thousand young people, utterly denouncing nuclear weapons, their possession and use. He even went so far as to advocate the death penalty for anyone using nuclear weapons, regardless of their nationality, or whether they were victorious or defeated.

As a Buddhist, Toda believed implicitly in the sanctity of life; and he was in no way supporting the death penalty as a general means of punishment. But he made such a strong statement because he wanted to powerfully drive home the point that nuclear weapons are an absolute evil. He wanted to root out the very tendency or devilish nature within peoples' minds that could even attempt to justify the use of nuclear weapons.

The people of the world have an inviolable right to live, he stated; and the SGI has continued to promote the intent of his declaration to the world.

YOUTH

What are you young people going to do?

It's up to you. Each and every one of you has the potential to turn the world around. These are no mere idle, dreamy words. You have that power.

To live in a society, in a world, where a handful of inept, cowardly usurpers of power plot your future and tell you what you can or cannot do, is a mockery. It is totally and completely unacceptable.

I say, rise up, displaying your inalienable rights and power.

The people are the true superpower. Do not give away your power. No one has the right to possess the key that will annihilate you and your mother and father and brothers and sisters around the globe. What kiind of insanity is this?

Governments do not deserve to stand which preach absolute power over the people. Leaders do not deserve to stand who attempt to selfishly garner and exercise unlimited power over the people.

No one has the right to push the button that will annihilate millions of innocents. No one has that right.

Cut this evil thinking at its root.

And resist anyone who justifies such destruction with passages and lies from any book or prophecy. Burn in a pile any such books or prophecies, castigate any such corruption of justice and morality.

This world is indeed a madhouse, a world on fire, a burning bush in the wind; but souls have become beacons and lighthouses before, lighting a way to the future, and you must become one of them also.

Youth! Stand up!

Seize the initiative for a new world!

Become one of those who forego the lures of power and money and fame and position, to serve the people. Serve the people in any way you can, simple or grandiose. Then you will find your true self, you will know who you are, you will open up your own life and the life of those around you.

Be as great as you can be. Never listen to those who proclaim that things are impossible. You will never know what is possible until you put your shoulder to the wheel and try with all your might.

No half-hearted measures! Boldly carve out your future. When you fuse your life with the unfolding life of the universe, with its heart, you will know with certainty that nothing is impossible.

Make the world a mirror of your intent.

Billions upon billions of ages of men and women have brought you to this point. Now, for their sake, fear nothing. Stride forth fearlessly among the wreckage, among the hopelessness and despair, among the gathering chaos, among your sisters and brothers and mothers and fathers and sons and daughters imploring you, praying for you to boldly lead the way.

The heavens rejoice in your ascent.

THE CEREMONY OF LIFE

Even in life, death is all around us. Stars are born and die, grass grows then withers; winter turns to spring, turns to summer, to autumn, and back again to winter. Nothing stays. Our life today will vanish tomorrow.

We live in a time when we have no answers anymore. Those who think they have the answers are especially the ones who have no answers. They are like dead leaves on dying branches.

Chaos is growing, like a whirling tornado drawing everything into its spinning maw.

Where is the meaning in all of this?

The child who was bombed in Beirut or Afghanistan or Iraq, or who died a slow disintegrating death of drugs or utter loss of hope in Chicago or Atlanta or New York - where is the meaning?

After the hurricane destruction in New Orleans, a prominent preacher was asked why God had allowed it to happen. He did not know.

From the old religions, there is no longer any anwer at all.

This is the universe where now appears the Bomb.

Equal in might - even millions of times mightier - is the solitary self.

Why did the bomb even appear if there was not some gathering force, a new and bold potential, about to emerge from the human heart.

What is necessary to make the change - that quantum leap into the new, emerging future of the human race? It is one person alone.

Boundless is the as yet unrevealed power in the mind and heart of a single human being. The solitary self rules the universe and the colliding monsters of galaxies devouring each other in intergalactic time and space and the trillions of universes unknown beyond our own, and the suns unnumbered spawning and dying out of dark black gravitational holes.

It is time for that person to take center stage. It is a time for laughter and revelation. It is a time of great spiritual transformation.

To feel the universe speakiing through your own voice and mind, to find stars in your vision and feel the pulsing of deep energy flowing and surging up from within. To know who you are. To move unerringly. To remember all that has gone before and treasure all memories, all greatness, all the love of mothers, all those unremembered and forgotten, all their voices and dreams, and to carry all this forth upon the wave of the birthing dream of Life itself.

At last, we discover who we are.

We are the great eternal ceremony of Life emerging from the dark Earth, bells ringing; solemn yet joyous, dancing, eternal.

We are becoming who we were meant to be. We are becoming who we were all along.

These are the beginnings of the great Springtime.

THE BATTLE

I must work on myself once again.

Conflicted with darkness and light, now raging, now filled with joy.

To look into the hearts of others and find myself there. To feel. To be aware of life's potential. To be strong. To depend on no one and nothing. To give, when I feel like taking. To summon up joy and courage out of depression and doubt and discouragement. To battle my self-imposed limits. To be kinder. To remember throughout time and space all those who have lent me support. To cultivate mercy for those who tested me and made me grow. To be aware of my own and others' greatness.

To never give in. To realize dreams.

I must work on myself once again.

A BEAUTIFUL DREAM

Nothing can defeat a beautiful dream.

During the second world war, in Nazi Germany, at the height of Hitler's madness and power, there was a small group of students at the University in Munich who had a dream.

They dreamt of a free world, they dreamt of a Europe that was united and at peace.

Their dream must have seemed utter madness to others, yet they held to it, nurtured it together, these handful of young idealists and dreamers. They met secretly to talk and write. They called themselves the Weisse Rose, or White Rose.

They could have been silent; but they began composing leaflets addressed to the German people, which they secretly posted on walls all over Munich.

In their leaflets, they tried to awaken the German people to the horrors that were going on at the battle fronts and elsewhere. They encouraged the German people to rise up and overthrow Hitler and the Nazis.

A handful of students in other cities joined the White Rose, and the letters began appearing there also, on walls, strewn here and there on pavements.

The Nazis were incensed. This was at the height of their oppressive power. Hitler was envisioning a thousand year Third Reich. There was no room to breathe. Death, or a living death awaited anyone resisting. Millions of men, women and children were being carted off to work camps and gas chambers.

Yet these fragile blooms of children asserted themselves. They stood up where no one else would stand up. Their pleas and leaflets fell on astoundingly deaf ears, yet they continued their secret work.

Eventually, they were discovered and betrayed, and almost all of them, these young students, were executed, were beheaded.

The Nazi machinery of death rolled on - itself, in the end, also utterly destroyed.

The White Rose survived though. The White Rose not only survived, but is today known throughout all of Europe, honored by an older generation and by generations of young people all over the continent and all over the world.

These few members of the White Rose are indeed heroes and heroines - not only for their extraordinary courage, but for something else...

The dream they nourished came true.

One of the few survivors, Franz Muller, explains:

> "The question is: Why is the White Rose, which was a very small group - altogether perhaps fifty people - why is this group so famous?

> "The answer is simple: Because we produced six leaflets against the war, against the Nazis - AND, it's always forgotten - at the end of the fifth leaflet, we made a prophecy of a new world, especially a new Europe, exactly what we see here today, a unified Europe of slowly coming together States, as the Americans did two hundred years before..

> "We made this prophecy in this leaflet number five that there will come a united Europe and a free Europe and a democratic Europe. We were resistance people, but also people who had a prophecy and a message for our country.

> "And it's a real satisfaction for me and for the few of us who are still living - three or four, the youngest of the White Rose - that what we wanted, what we wrote and hoped for, and that for which we suffered, slowly, but very surely has come into reality."

THE SPIRIT OF THE LAND

I remember. Nothing is forgotten.
Faces of the children and of mothers long suffering.
The Indians who knew the land, who spoke
with the clouds and mountains and rushing streams.
I remember. I am the spirit of the land.

Vortexes of water rise from off the oceans,
washing away dessication and debris.
Glacial caps melt and move ponderously,
flowing south.
The fish and the birds and the bison reappear.

This is my land once again. I reappear.
A cataclysm swallows whole coasts,
creates tides that smash the old hubris,
the ancient undeserved pride.
My sun swaggers in the skies.
This is my land, I reclaim it once again.
Oh, hear my cry!

And the people arise.
The innocent, the children, the lost,
the long-suffering, the kindly, the simple,
the unadorned.
You and I.
Our mothers and fathers who cried
their hearts out for a better world,
who cried under the whip,
under the pain and labor of
interminable, difficult days,
waiting and hoping and enduring
and enduring and enduring,
beyond enduring.

SURMOUNTING DEATH

Mr. Akihiro Takahashi
Hiroshima survivor, age 74.

"One of our most powerful talents as human beings, they say, is our ability to forget. But I have never forgotten for a moment the horror of that day. And when my thoughts turn to this subject, I am forced to realize that August sixth marked the real starting point of my life.

"I have survived, but my right elbow and all the fingers except the thumb on my right hand are bent out of shape. I have keloid burns on both arms and legs, and a black nail continues to grow on my right index finger. I am afflicted also with chronic hepatitis. I have been hospitalized twelve times since 1971 and am still undergoing trreatment. I suffer from many other ailments as well.

"I fear for my life every day and, at times, my frail health has brought me close to despair. I

65

have often wondered, 'Why should I go on suf-fering like this?' But each time I remember that I survived. In this way I have lived until today.

"Hiroshima is not merely an historical fact. It is a continuous warning and lesson for the future. War is caused by human beings, and it leads not only to one's own death but to the deaths of loved ones, parents, brothers and sisters, teachers, and friends. A nuclear war, in partic-ular, has neither winners nor losers. It holds in store nothing less than the extinction of the human species, the effective destruction of the planet itself. If human beings don't eliminate nuclear weapons, then the weapons will surely eliminate us.

"Nuclear war, I believe, is truly a challenge to human reason and ideals. Human beings should abolish nuclear weapons and thus cre-ate world peace. We should transcend all pain, sadness and hatred from the past, join hands with each other regardless of differences of race or national boundaries, and change the flow of history from distrust to trust, from hos-tility to reconciliation, and from division to har-mony.

"One person's strength is limited, of course, but no one is completely powerless. Unless some-one starts something, we will have nothing. I firmly believe that peace can come about only through the cumulative efforts of individual citi-zens everywhere.

"Peace will not simply be handed to us as a gift; it will not come walking up to greet us; and, finally, it will not arrive if we simply sit and wait. Peace is something we must create, something we must actively talk about, act on, build upon, and then strive to make happen.

"World peace will not arrive at a stroke. We have to build peace from where we are, beginning right around us. In other words, we must begin in our homes, in our schools, in our workplaces, in our communities. Then, standing on that foundation, we can bring peace to the world.

"We need to eliminate nuclear weapons from the world. We need to make the world truly peaceful. In order to do so, I want young people to inherit and be aware of our experiences and to work for a peaceful world.

"There are a lot of negative legacies of the 20th century, such as war, nuclear weapons, terrorism, global warming, famine, refugees, oppression of human rights and violence. It was us adults who created this negative legacy.

"To make the world peaceful, each person needs to make an effort. Don't think that one person cannot make a difference. Each person has power. Each person has to do something. If a person does nothing, that equals zero. By one person taking action, things start to move or change.

"From one person to a second to a third, fourth and fifth, let's make a circle of peace and spread it. That's what I really want to tell younger people. If you're just waiting for peace to come, it doesn't come to you. Peace is something we make and create. We cannot win the peace unless we are actively involved.

"In order to do so, let's have courage. Let's challenge ourselves and make effort. Let's not ignore the power we have. Let's bring forth the power we have and direct it toward peace.

"I hope the younger generations will make Hiroshima their starting point and view the world from a more global perspective. To that end, and to make the 21st century a century of light and hope, I intend to continue to devote whatever energy I have left to telling my experience and spreading the spirit of Hiroshima."

JUSTICE

The heart of the universe itself is justice.

Justice always has and always will prevail. There is nothing that does not yield its own reward. The heart and its workings will always and forever prevail.

A grand and just effort, even if it ends in death, in obscurity, carries on forever - adds to the fragrance of the universe.

The aiding of others, the soft encouraging word, the caring, the battling of injustice and arrogance and misuse of power - these never end in nothingness. It is a gathering wind that blows now softly, now loud, that rises in the end toward new beginnings and great ends and honors all those who have given of their strength and courage to bring forth new life. Such words, such deeds, never die, they are remembered forever, they become part and parcel of new shoots and branches rising forever from the great pulsing heart of the universe.

Who am I? Where have I been? Where am I going?

I am that which has been here forever.

I appear and make my mark and fade from view, but nothing is ever lost. The waves crest on the ocean, then recede to where they came; but nothing is ever lost. The ocean remains. No great effort of the heart is ever lost.

WOMEN

It is the time for women. Too long have women waited in the shadows, ignored, unrecognized for their greatness.

Women are the nurturers of life.

Give ordinary women the reins of power and they will think twice and thrice before sending their children into war.

Women are the natural proponents of dialogue. Dialogue is what is needed in the world today, true dialogue, careful listening, accommodating the other into one's own world, exchanging worldviews and growing from the exchange. Women need to extend the power of their compassion and dialogue into every arena of life.

Women have power. Women have endurance.

Gandhi, who led the revolution that changed India, valued women as the mainstay of his movement. He stated:

> "To know that a woman is more than a man is
> in itself true education."

ROOTS

A debate still rages about whether America was founded upon Christian principles, that this nation's bedrock was Christianity.

The American Indians would certainly take exception to this view. They were certainly closer to the truth. But even then, this would only be a shallow perspective.

The real spiritual roots of America, whose branches will spread out endlessly into the future, was a spirituality which extended back vast aeons into the past. It came long before Christ, and was the bedrock upon which Jesus himself forged his life and thoughts.

Ralph Waldo Emerson, Henry David Thoreau, Walt Whitman - the writers and poets of the American Renaissance - these were the ones who gave expression to our national psyche and soul, they laid the cornerstone, and these were the prophets who resurrected our true heritage.

In the January 1844 issue of the Dial, the publication of the New England Transcendentalist Club, Thoreau introduced a translation of the "Parable of the Medicinal Herbs" chapter of the Lotus Sutra, the core and heart of all Buddhist teachings.

There was no mistake; the ties were deep and inscrutable.

Thoreau, along with Emerson and Whitman - these prophets who upheld a profound vision of America, who sang ancient tunes composed in a new language - appeared at precisely the perfect moment for the birth of this land. Their words came from a place that flows on untouched forever. It is the Truth.

Emerson recognized this Truth. He perceived it in his own life and in the lives of ordinary people, each and every one. His was a war against the lies that diverted peoples' eyes away - like an enchanted mirror - from the Truth: that each man and each woman possesses the power of God within himself or herself, that all things, good and evil, emanate from the human heart and mind. His was a battle to restore power to the individual, to wrest power away from the old gods, the usurpers, the priests, the intermediaries, the innate powers of darkness and illusion. His was a self and an individuality anchored in eternity.

America's connection with this Truth is deep.

We walk around, move by others day by day, and we never notice, never notice the rivers running deep beneath our feet. We have met each other before. Lincoln spoke of the "mystic chords of memory."

Whitman sang:

> "I am the mate and companion of people, all just as
> immortal and fathomless as myself;
> They do not know how immortal, but I know."

These prophets sensed, beneath ordinary events and lives, the grand mosaic and chorus of Life.

The Lotus Sutra, introduced by Thoreau to America, is the grand chorus of Life itself.

In the Lotus Sutra, Shakyamuni Buddha assembles around himself on Eagle Peak in India his vast array of disciples.

After forty years of preaching, he is at last about to reveal the Truth.

Shakyamuni reveals to all those present that, contrary to what everyone believed - that he had achieved his enlightenment at about age thirty while seated in meditation beneath a bodhi tree - he had actually reached enlightenment at an immensely remote time in the past, a time beyond conception; and had ever since been present in the world preaching the Lotus Sutra and opening up the Way to myriads of others.

Then, as he was speaking, from the Earth itself there rose up a gigantic jewel-encrusted Treasure Tower. Shakyamuni seated himself in this Tower, which was half the size of the Earth itself, and the great Treasure Tower rose up into the air; and lo and behold, countless myriads of great beings - Bodisattvas - emerged from out of the Earth, shining and resplendent and beyond number, and took their place in this great assembly.

Was this assembly a figment of someone's imagination? No, it was real. It happened, and it did not happen.

It was the emergence of a great state of Life from within the life of Shakyamuni himself. It was the great dormant, unrecognized state of Life inherent in us all given brilliant expression and manifestation.

The myriads of resplendent great beings - Bodisattvas - were then entrusted by Shakyamuni with the mission of opening up the lives of all people in the future to this vast state of life, this Treasure Tower within. They would come forth and emerge when the time had arrived.

Thoreau opened the door to their entrance in America.

They now appear. They appear as no one special, as men and women immersed in the suffering of this world.

Yet in their hearts and in their true identity, they are the fore-runners of a new race of humanity. They bring joy, they bring power, and they bring forth a wealth of compassion for all living beings that can be defeated by nothing.

They awaken the true meaning of America.

They are here; they are everywhere; unannounced.

They are you and I.

THE DAWN

We need a fresh breeze blowing across this land. We need to clear out all the dead branches in the trees, and make way for new shoots. Too long we have been in autumn and winter, now the spring needs to usher forth with unsurpassed brilliance.

We have been lost for too long here in America. The poets despaired of death and carnage, the devastating blows to the heart. Justice seemed lost.

But justice is never lost. The heart and trajectory of the universe itself is justice. All will come around.

What is needed is a great new vision, an awakening to utter reality. This is coming. You may not see it, looking around this bruised planet, the deepening bloodshed and violence and fracturing of the heart. But it is coming.

It is always darkest before the dawn.

We are progenitors of the dawn.

A REAL LADY

She was born in 1906 in St. Louis, Missouri, as Frieda McDonald. Raised in a poor black family, she dropped out of school at the age of twelve, and was performing on stage at age thirteen.

At age nineteen, she went to Paris and, almost overnight, became a tremendous sensation as a dancer and singer. Her name now was Josephine Baker.

Until her death in 1975, she was a living legend. She was one of the highest paid entertainers in Europe.

During the second world war, she fought on the side of the resistance and was a spy for France. She deeply loved her adopted country. She told the military authorities: "Do with me what you wish."

She hid arms in her home, and had a radio receiver there also, with which she communicated with General DeGaulle in London. She had coded messages encrypted into her music. She took Jewish refugees into her troup, most of whom were due to be deported to concentration camps. For any of these efforts, she could have lost her life.

In the 1950's she began adopting poor children from other countries, until she had an even dozen. She called them her "Rainbow Tribe". She called her home her "World Village."

When Josephine returned to the United States to perform, she met a solid wall of racism. She refused to perform to segregated audiences, and because of this, she lost a lot of money. But she didn't care. It only motivated her to begin a lifelong struggle against racial discrimination. In 1963, she was at the side of Martin Luther King, Jr., in the march on Washington.

At her funeral in Paris, 20,000 people gathered to pay their respects. She was the first America woman buried in France with military honors.

Josephine was truly a great lady. She was also a great world citizen.

At the core of her life was a passion for living, and a fierce determination to show the entire world that there exists but one race, the human race.

JOE

Joe was my best friend. He died in 2006, age 79, from complications of heart surgery.

Joe had such a bright, brilliant manner. He was a wonderful writer, and for twenty-five years he lived and wrote screenplays in Paris.

He loved France. Even after he returned to Los Angeles with his French wife Framboise, and lived out his last fifteen years there, he used to tell me that he dreamt every night of being back at the cafes in Paris.

Joe was Jewish, and having suffered discrimination himself, he would not tolerate discrimination of others.

I could describe many things that I feel in my heart about Joe; but I want to relate just two stories about Joe that reflect what kind of person he was.

Just before his 50th high school reunion in Los Angeles, Joe found out that a large number of his classmates would not be there. They were a large group of Japanese-Americans who had been interned in prison camps during the second world war. As a result, these men and women had been unable to graduate from high school, and had never received their diplomas.

Joe went to work.

He called the TV stations, he called the newspapers and radio stations. He contacted the school authorities. He found out where these Japanese-American classmates of his were then living. By himself, he created a PR campaign that aroused everyone in his old community, that ended with these classmates of his receiving - belatedly - their high school diplomas at the reunion. The media covered the event and it was all over the news programs in Los Angeles.

Most moved by his efforts were the Japanese-Americans who had been so unjustly imprisoned during their high school years. It was the closure of some deeply held wounds.

The second story involved the famous writer, Maya Angelou.

Maya had been turned down when trying to rent an apartment in Los Angeles because of her race. It was an obvious case of discrimination.

Again, Joe - who happened to know Maya - went to work.

He applied for the apartment himself, and was promptly accepted. Later in the day, he accompanied Maya, with her belongings, to the apartment. The landlord was furious. He swore at Joe, calling him everything in the book.

Joe, though, did not back down. He countered with a verbal assault on the landlord, accusing him of being a fascist bastard, and threatening to take him to court. The landlord was furious, but had to back down, and Maya moved into her new apartment.

This is documented in one of her books.

In countries all over the world, how many ruthless dictators and monsters would not have come to power and committed their atrocities, if people like Joe - with his fearlessness in standing up to injustice - had been around?

FATHER AND SON

I met a young man today - someone in their late twenties - who has a son.

This young man attended college for a few years, but never had the finances to continue on. His dream was to be a journalist.

The dream has faded now, though, and he has had difficulty making a living. It has come to the point that, in order to support his son and give him some kind of stable future, he has enlisted in the military. This is the only way he can now see to open up his future. He may be fed for cannonfodder to war, leaving his young son alone, but this is the only way he can see to move ahead.

What kind of society have we become that the future of young men and young women has to be encased in war and death? What kind of leaders have we promoted - what have we ourselves done - to create a society where this young man has to march off to hell and murder and war to support his infant son?

What kind of world have we become?

REALITY

Only a few weeks before Hiroshima, the first ever atomic bomb was detonated at the Trinity test site in central New Mexico.

Robert Oppenheimer, chief scientist in charge of the development of the bomb, was there that day.

At the moment the bomb detonated, he recalled the ancient Indian words of the Hindu god Vishnu as that god attempted to threaten a human being into following his dictates. To intimidate the human, Vishnu re-formed himself into the visage of an immense multi-armed writhing figure.

"Now I am become Death," he told the human, "destroyer of worlds."

In New Mexico that fateful day, it was Death and the destruction of all of life and utter and incomprehensible and overwhelming evil that showed its visage that day to all human beings on the planet.

No more hiding. Just a hideous reality.

"Now I am become Death, destroyer of worlds."

It was indeed a pivotal point in human history. We came face to face that day with our own power to annihilate the human race.

On that day, what the bomb instilled into the human psyche was a deep and all-pervading sense of powerlessness.

One of the survivors of the Hiroshima bomb described it thus:

> "The powerlessness of not being able to help or participate because we didn't know what dropped. Even those people who didn't have any burns and injuries started to suffer and drop dead because, you know, the radiation, how forceful it was there.

> "It goes into the marrow of your bones and penetrates your brains and then changes your fetus, and malformed children are born. We had no idea how to help ourselves or help anybody. So that kind of death is annihilation and death without dignity. Complete powerlessness. Not even a person being there, torturing you. It's invisible. Done to people, DNA, plants."

That individual people - handfuls of people - have the power to initiate this kind of utter and absolute destruction - this is the greatest of all insanities. That a few people - who knows why; because they have risen to the top of a demented political or military establishment - possess the power, this moment, to push buttons or insert codes that will launch monsters of destruction hurtling on their way to you and I and hundreds of millions of other human beings all over the planet - is this not insane abdication of power from the many to the few?

Where are the wills of ordinary people in this eerie scenario? Our power has been totally subsumed by malignant warheads.

Do you know what we are daily facing, even today?

There are literally thousands of deadly machines aimed at you and I this very moment. These missiles remain, after decades of detente, poised on hair-trigger alert launch status both in the United States and Russia.

Thousands of these messengers of death remain pointed obscenely at your life; and more and more of their control is being turned over to computers, where one glitch, one wrong or accidental move, one miscalculation, and literally millions will die.

Do you think the annihilation done at Hiroshima and Nagasaki was horrific? Yes, it was. It was beyond imagining.

And yet, those bombs are as nothing compared to the weapons now poised at your heart and mine, at your city and mine.

Missiles on launch status in the United States and Russia now hold multiple bombs each - each one capable of producing destruction a thousand times more horrific than Hiroshima. One bomb capable of producing a thousand Hiroshimas in just seconds. Can you imagine a thousand Hiroshimas obliterating your life and your city?

What happens when a bomb like that goes off?

On March 1st, 1954, the United States detonated a hydrogen bomb on Bikini Atoll in the Pacific, one of many such tests. The magnitude of the explosion was unexpected even by the scientists running the test. The bomb oblliterated an island, tore apart the ecosystem on a huge scale, and spread radioactive fallout over 7000 square miles. Even 100 miles east of Bikini, Marshall Islanders were exposed to the fallout and are still suffering to this day from the effects of the bomb.

Tony de Brum, a former senator of the Marshall Islands, was a young boy when the bomb went off.

> "On the morning of March 1st, I was doing what other youngsters were doing in my village. I was carrying a fish basket for my grandfather, who was net-throwing for small schools of fish that swam around our beaches, in the early dawn hours.

> "Without warninig, a sudden flash went off - a flash that I still cannot describe to this day. It was as if someone had walked up to you with a hundred flashbulbs and shot them at your eyes. We were all temporarily blinded, all of us, including the other grandfathers or uncles or dads who were doing similar types of fishing on the beach.

> "And then, to this day I do not know what came first or how long it was between the sequence of events...but a shock...and then the whole sky began to take on an eerie crimson color. I describe it as if someone had put a glass bowl over all of us and poured blood over it.

> "I can still hear my grandfather saying 'run, run,

"run. I wanted to ask him also what was happening , but I could not run and neither could I speak. The image that was implanted in my brain on that morning remains with me to this day.

"Bravo, alone, the March 1st test that I just described to you, was equivalent to one thousand Hiroshima shots. One thousand Hiroshima shots. And if you took the yield of all sixty-seven shots that were detonated in the Marshallls between 1946 and 1958, you would have the equivalent of 1.6 Hiroshima shots every day for twelve years."

This is what man did to the earth and to people and to animals and fishes and birds and whole islands - islands that are still unlivable. This is what man did to the earth on which he lives and draws his sustenance.

This is not an abstraction. This is not a Nintendo game.

Young people, especially: This is a reality. This is your world.

This is a monster that has arisen from the darkest depths of the waters of life.

Oblilteration. Nothingness. A nothingness beyond nothingness. No life. The end of life.

Even as we think we have mastered these bombs and harnessed their power, and not one nuclear weapon has been dropped on human beings since Hiroshima, this monster we have unleased has penetrated our bones and marrow and nerves and brains, seeping into the very core of our life.

As long as these weapons exist, they will eventually be used. As long as human beings believe in these weapons and possess these weapons and give power to these weapons, they will be used.

These weapons come from the darkest part of the universe itself. They come from the darkest part of our own hearts.

Physically, we face threats that are like ticking bombs.

Psychically, something has been poisoned in our greater, collective life.

In Buddhism, there is a term called esho funi. It means two, but not two. In the depths of life, everything is basically interconnected.

The environment, ourselves, other people, the sun and moon and oceans - are all, in reality, inseparable.

This is also the truth established by quantum physics.

What is without is mirroring that which is within. The pollution, the environmental devastation, the wars, the divisions and fracturing of peoples and nationalities, the meltdown of the world - all are mirroring the pollution, the devastation, the divisions, hatreds and greed within the collective human heart.

We can drop bomb after bomb in an attempt to annihilate our enemies; but the truth is that in so doing we are destroying our own hearts.

The truth is, we are connected to the environment. It is our life itself. As we destroy and maim and pollute and devastate the environment, we destroy and maim and devastate our own inner life.

The world is our mirror. The universe is our mirror.

There is no escaping. There is no escaping the truth of Life. As you do unto others, so it will be done unto you.

The world - and your own inner world - exists in inescapable bondage to the law of cause and effect.

When will we see our image in the mirror? When will we awaken and see ourselves in the mirror of eternity?

This is the age we live in. This is the moment of reckoning.

We are imprisoned by the power of thousands of bombs, and tiny buttons and signals and ignorant, unenlightened men who may at any moment initiate our doom. This is the demonic reality behind all the show, the day-to-day banalities, the hidden agenda that rules our psyche.

Does it matter? Do millions of men and women and children really matter?

Does one human being really matter?

A NATION'S GREATNESS

For too long we have measured our greatness in terms of money, or military power, or gross economic indexes. These are no true measures of greatness at all. It is time we have done with them.

The measure of a people or a nation should be its capacity for humanistic action.

How much suffering have we alleviated? How much happiness have we given to our own people and to people around the globe? How much sickness have we eradicated? What beachheads of peace and progress have we created? What have we done for the betterment of the world?

BLACK AND WHITE

Nelson Mandela survived twenty-seven years in a jail cell.

Have you spent even one day and night in jail? Twenty-seven years was truly an eternity.

The incomprehensible thing is how he managed to maintain his humanity amid this desert of timelessness.

He wielded a heavy hammer for years in the hot blazing South African sun cracking limestone blocks. Those blocks were apartheid, ruled over by a white minority, given meaning and legitimacy by the Christian Church.

After twenty-seven years of cracking limestone blocks, the rock of apartheid itself cracked, and the tide turned. Mandela himself became President of his country.

On the very day he was sworn into office, Mandela invited his jailkeeper to the ceremonies. Such was the magnimanity of his heart, such was his love of the people. He embraced even his enemies.

Rosa Parks, a simple black woman, refused to give up her seat on a bus to a white man. She was tired. She was tired physically, and she was tired spiritually of the degradation of herself and her people. She refused to move; and a movement was born. From this one woman's courage, thousands followed. A crack appeared in the edifice of white power and legitimacy.

Martin Luther King, Jr. had a dream; and streams of similar pent-up, previously obstructed dreams broke loose and flowed into his dream; and his dream became a mighty raging river which cracked the dam of racism and hatred and filled the future with innumerable dreams where they had not been possible before.

These were only three; but many followed. They were black, and the world was white.

Where would we all be without these courageous black brothers and sisters? What kind of people would we still be?

OUR DUTY

Gandhi lived the life he spoke of. He lived it with his life. His was an unparalleled example.

He once stated:

> "Civilization in the real sense of the term consists not in the multiplication, but in the deliberate and voluntary reduction of, wants. This alone promotes real happiness and contentment and increases the capacity for service."

And again:

> "I hold myself incapable of hating any being on earth. By a long course of prayerful discipline, I have ceased for over forty years to hate anybody."

Some one once found him writing with a pencil that had been worn down to a nub. He was offered a new one, but Gandhi refused, saying he had to use up the pencil completely because it had been purchased with the hard-earned money of his supporters, many of whom were very poor.

He was always concerned with the suffering of the people. He stated:

> "In India we have three million people who have to be satisfied with one meal a day, and that meal consists of a chapati containing no fat in it and a pinch of salt. You and I have no right to anything we have until these three millions are clothed and fed better. You and I, who ought to know better, must adjust our wants, and even undergo voluntary starvation in order that they be nursed, fed, and clothed."

How many of us - you and I together - have lived the phrases we harbor deep within our hearts?

END-TIME

Youth! What do you think this life is about? The show, the glitter, the elbowing for position and glory and fame and money - is that a life?

When time passes, and the real meaning of all that you have done and experienced becomes finally manifest, nothing, but nothing, will remain whatsoever but the memory of how you have fought, how you have struggled for justice and given of yourself for a great cause.

Peace and the happiness of others is a great cause.

Live so that when you come to the end of your journey, the faces of innumerable smiling faces crowd your memory, and your life drops down like a golden, rich, ripe apple from the tree of life.

LEADERSHIP

Leaders whose hearts are frozen hard to the sufferings and plights of the people are deserving of nothing but our utmost contempt. Leaders who manipulate the people and the passions of the people for their own power and gain, are deserving of nothing but our utmost contempt.

Let us lay down this rule for leadership: Leaders are here for no other purpose than the happiness of the people. Leaders are servants of the people.

Any leader who violates this rule deserves to be relegated to the ashbin of history.

THE REAL AMERICA

Even if we lose everything here in America that we have known up to this moment in time - the vast economic superiority, the money, the arrogance of power, the thousands of nuclear weapons, the tanks, the submarines, the stealth bombers, the opulence, television and big sports games and mega shopping malls - America and Americans can still be the greatest in the world, we can be the stars of a new era, the forerunners of a vision of life and of the heart that has never unfolded before in history. This is our true mission here in these fifty states. We are here to give voice and presence to the great dream that has lain dormant and suppressed and buried and trod upon for ages and millennia in the heart of humanity - the dream of equality and justice and compassion, the dream of a New World, this world that has escaped our grasp from the dawn of time but which refuses to die because it is the only true world, and it is a world which is imminently realizeable. This is the great dream of America which is ours to realize.

LIFE AND DEATH

We are afraid of the Bomb. We are afraid of Death.

America buries both, Death and the Bomb, in the deepest recesses of our memory.

We do not want to face either in this land of America. We would rather watch the Monday night football game, and the Tuesday night baseball game, and Saturday afternoon golf, and on and on, filling up the moment with distractions and happy hours and a whirlwind of trifling actions to keep the inevitable End at bay.

We do not want to hear of Death. We will live forever. We take another pill and exercise more and find a new cure, while millions of deaths taking place all over the globe are filed away in some drawer.

The Bomb does not go away, though. Death does not go away.

We thought we were through with all that; but now the bombs are back, proliferating and spreading everywhere. Like a mutating virus, they creep back, more deadly than ever, resistant to everything we can muster against them. Soon the megadeath bomb will slide by everyone's notice in a briefcase.

(We are not alone. Our brothers and sisters now number six billion in the mirror).

Death and the Bomb are even now seeping ever deeper into our lives.

All over this country lie pools of Death, waste products of nuclear weapons and nuclear power.

Plutonium 239, one of these elements, is extraordinarily deadly to humans, even in microscopic amounts. Plutonium 239 has a half-life of 24,000 years. This means this deadly element will be around threatening our existence for at least a quarter of a million years.

These wastes will not just disappear. They will not go away. They are connected integrally to our very blood stream now.

(Our hearts have spawned these deadly wastes)

At Hanford, Washington, where the first atomic bombs were developed, billions of dollars have been spent trying to contain these wastes. The government has claimed in the past that these wastes were being stored in containers that would be safe for 10,000 years; yet, even now, plutonium 239 has begun to leach into the soil, making its way to the Columbia River - a river that flows into others rivers and tributaries affecting millions of lives. This is a time bomb waiting to happen.

We do not know how to handle these wastes.

The plan is to store them in a giant underground vault at Yucca Mountain, Nevada.

Even if we do, however, the amount of waste this vault can hold would only perhaps cover the amount of waste existing at current commercial nuclear power plants. It would not cover the wastes existing at military sites, such as Hanford; and it would also not allow for the storage of wastes in the future from our currently existing power plants, not to mention the wastes that would be produced if new power plants come on line.

We are dealing here with a problem that is going to be around for a very, very long time. How can we be sure of safely containing these wastes for the short term - let alone the next few hundred thousand years?

In the mean time, we continue to develop nuclear weapons, and we continue to expand our plans for the development of more nuclear power plants.

Like the Bomb itself, like Death, we refuse to face up to realities. We enjoy electricity created by these nuclear power plants, and we enjoy the illusion of safety of thousands of nuclear weapons.

But what about the future? What about our chilrden? Do we really care about our children or their future?

We are placing a horrible burden directly upon them. We are creating for them - out of our own comfort - a diminished future.

It is necessary that we face ourselves.

Death gives meaning to it all. Death is the twin brother and sister of Life, and both dwell in eternity. Death awakens us to who we truly are. The Bomb is here to awaken us to who we truly are.

We are one with each other. We are all a part of Life. Every deed we put forth has reverberations that affect the course of the universe.

Everything reflected in the mirror is ourselves. We have to awaken to this Truth.

The Bomb will force us to do that. If we do not change, if we do not grow beyond ourselves and come to recognize the unity of Life, we will all without fail irrevocably perish.

The hibakusha, the survivors of the hell and death of Hiroshima and Nagasaki, know this. They could have taken two paths.

One is the path of defeat, of defeat as a human being, a spiraling down into hatred and self-pity and the hellishness of life. The other - the path of Life - took much, much more courage, just as a struggle for peace requires infinitely more courage and manhood and womanhood than war ever demands.

It was a struggle wrought from the deepest recesses of the soul and heart, a display of endurance beyond any capacity to endure, a cry of affirmation arising from utter desolation.

Above all, it was a call to a new level of being. Henceforth, these survivors would never function in the same old ways anymore. Their eyes were opened to heaven and hell.

It was an utter overcoming of the small, provincial self, an ushering into the light and knowledge of what it means to live upon this Earth among countless suns and moons and stars.

We are all one, and they know it now.

Amid the daily pain, they rise each day to awaken others - the world - to the horror they experienced and to a message of Life and peace issuing forth not from some platform of weakness and ineffectual words and futile gestures, but from an incredibly intense effort of compassion and will.

These are truly world citizens. They are truly to be honored.

They have come, slowly, to embody the force that will defeat the Bomb.

WHAT'S IT ALL ABOUT?

The days pass by; triumphs and deceits, loss and gain, people, friends, a thousand, thousand faces of strangers passing by us on the streets; memories of childhood, of innocence; and volcanic eruptions, war, devastation, hungry children in the streets, money lost or won; the common, daily gestures; mothers and fathers and brothers and sisters; our struggles to win, to gain some sort of recognition; things said or left unsaid, things done or left undone; and the hurts, and the loves, and all those millions and millions of things that seemed so important; and then the end of days and looking back and suddenly seeing ourselves not there anymore, just the night and the stars shining over the silent city and realizing suddenly what it all meant, did my life mean anything, did it leave an impact; or is it like silent falling snow obliterating tiny footprints, then no trace at all?

What is important is how much compassion we carry with us into the dark.

AWAKENING

They are the children of the universe.

People we thought ordinary, backward, simple, of not much consequence, waitresses, mechanics, shopkeepers, plumbers, accountants, factory workers, landscapers, farmers, field workers, telephone operators, maids, bellhops, boat builders, policemen, television repairmen, sales people, dressmakers, cooks, and on and on - all come forward now shedding their masks, removing the old clothes, stepping forth laughing and shining and dancing to bright tunes.

They emerge from the earth, from the simple life of the earth, from forever and ever, displaying their greatness.

Buddhas as far as the eye can see.

REVOLUTION

There is always - and always will be - a time for revolution.

Life moves on, and with it, change. Life never ceases developing. Always there is this urge to transcend the present, to move and expand towards a greater state of life, a greater self-awareness, a deeper and broader sense of compassion commensurate with the mind and heart of the universe itself.

We are the universe becoming one with itself.

THE PEOPLE

Where are the people? They are awakening. The nation as a whole is awakening to deafening realities - the dead lying in pools and ditches in desert towns, the monstrosity of twisted steel and hundreds of thousands of blighted lives as we watch the evening news and eat our dinners and listen to arguments pro and con and grow accustomed to our leaders' crooked smiles.

A day of reckoning is at hand. It has already arrived. It has buried its way into our hearts, and wormed its way into our off-spring. We have committed atrocities. We are guilty of lies and murder. We have murdered the future. We are awakening, awakening; yet still unable to boldly eye the murderer in the mirror.

FOREVER

Life will not prosper a narrow, partisan view of the universe. Life will not support injustice.

All that serves to sever, to compartmentalize, to segregate, to cut off the all-inclusive, all-embracing impetus of Life will never, in the long run, prosper. Not in a million, million years. Life will support and enhance that which expands and enhances the Life of the whole.

Life is always moving forward, always on the edge of change, always reaching for a greater inclusiveness. Life is always trying to bring forth an effulgence of flowers. Life is always trying to bloom beyond itself. More and more and more.

We are waiting for the true heroes to appear. One person can create a new world.

Her name was Isabella Baumfree.

She was born in 1797 in upstate New York, and spoke only Dutch until she was seven years old.

She was a slave, one of thirteen children born to slave parents. She was sold several times, and suffered a great deal under slavery. She was forced by her third master to marry an older man, with whom she had five children.

In 1843, she underwent a spiritual revelation, and took on the name of Sojourner Truth.

She spent much of the rest of her life traveling from town to town, preaching and speaking out against slavery and for womens' rights. Her preaching was fired by the indignities that she herself had suffered as a woman and as a slave.

During the Civil War, she raised food and clothing for black regiments, and met President Abraham Lincoln at the White House. While she was there, she challenged the policy of segregating street cars by race. A tireless fighter for human rights and a powerful speaker, she was perhaps the most famous African-American woman in the nineteenth century.

At one point, she met and became friends with Harriet Beecher Stowe, world famous as the author of the great anti-slavery novel, "Uncle Tom's Cabin."

Earlier, in 1851, Mrs. Stowe had been living on the campus of Bowdoin College in Brunswick, Maine, where her husband was teaching. The controversy over slavery was swirling and dividing the nation. She wrote:

> "Up to this year I have always felt that I had no particular call to meddle with this subject. But I feel now that the time is come when even a woman or a child who can speak a word for freedom and humanity is bound to speak."

And speak she did. Her novel, Uncle Tom's Cabin, documented in passionate and heart-rending detail the tragic breakup of black Kentucky families sold down the river to slavery. Almost overnight, the characters of Uncle Tom, Little Eva, and the villanous Simon Legree became household words.

In its first year, her book sold 300,000 copies - an enormous achievment at that time - and became an international best seller.

The main theme of her book was that slavery and Christianity cannot co-exist. She portrayed slavery as it was, a vast interlocking social system based on profit, with no regard for the human cost.

After the Civil War broke out, Mrs. Stowe visited the White House to urge President Abraham Lincoln to do something for the thousands of slaves who had fled north to the capitol. Lincoln greeted her as "the little woman who wrote the book that made this great war."

Her book did not actually start the Civil War, but it was enormously important in shaping public opinion on the slavery issue. She was only one woman; yet her courage and passion stirred the moral conscience of the entire nation.

During the years 1846 to 1848, the United States fought another war, this time with Mexico, which was widely criticized as unjust and an attempt to expand slavery.

Henry David Thoreau, who was conducting his famous experiment in simple living at the time at Walden Pond, refused to pay his poll tax, as a demonstration against a government that supported slavery and an unjust war.

He spent only one night in jail, but the experience so enraged him that he wrote his great essay, Civil Disobedience.

He asked:

> "How does it become a man to behave toward this American government today? I cannot for an instant recognize that political organization as my government which is the slave's government also."

In the future, his actions and this small essay would profoundly influence many others who shared Thoreau's intense desire for justice and freedom, including Mahatma Gandhi, who struggled so fiercely and non-violently for the independence of India. Martin Luther King, Jr. cited it often during the civil rights movement of the 1960's, as did the activists who protested the war in Vietnam.

Sojourner Truth, Harriet Beecher Stowe, and Henry David Thoreau - all simple individuals who stood up and let their voices be heard, and who, as a result, changed the course of their times.

They all had a voice, and they simply let it be heard.

Our times are the same as theirs.

Who will stand up and be counted? Where is the moral outcry? Where is the rage?

Just as slavery is incompatible with Christianity, so too are nuclear weapons. The wholesale slaughter of humanity, the invasion of foreign countries, is incompatible with Christianity.

Those who possess and intend to use nuclear weapons - as our leaders and government intend absolutely to do, given the appropriate circumstances - have nothing whatsoever to do with the core principles of Christianity as laid down by its founder two thousand years ago.

Are you a Christian? How can you stand by and not raise your voice against a government that holds and advocates, given the appropriate circumstances, the use of these weapons and indiscriminate war?

It is about time we looked at ourselves in the mirror. It is about time we took a good long hard look at who we are, and who we have become.

America, as a whole, is insular, and ignorant of other cultures. Often we are even proud of this fact.

As a whole, we are a people who are unwilling to look at ourselves in the mirror. Self-reflection is foreign to us. This is a major weakness.

The inability to self-reflect means that the image we have of ourselves is frozen in time, and is impervious to change. We fail to understand that only as we pay tribute to others, are we worthy of respect ourselves. That culture is great which opens itself to the natural diversity and wonder of all of life. We cut off the world and shore up the walls of our defences. It is a great shame and pettiness.

Break down the walls! Usher in the future!

What is required is a new revolution. We have had enough of the old ones - economic, political, social, war.

The solution - and the beachhead of all future assaults on the problems confronting the world - lies with a revolution within the hearts of human beings.

This is a revolution of nuclear proportions.

This is total revolution.

There is no philosopher throughout history who has considered it even possible. It was thought that great thinkers and great seers would lead the way.

But what is required is that ordinary men and women lead the way.

Again, philosophers and thinkers have not thought this possible, because they assumed some special gift was necessary; some rare capable individuals, above and beyond the masses of the people, were required to manage or force such a change.

You will see them coming. They are already here. They will grow to legions. It is a new world emerging.

The old forces, the old ways, grind themselves to dust.

Shortly before my mother died, when she was ill and breaking down physically, I asked her: "What would you like your life to be like the next time you live?"

She answered, unhesitatingly.

"To have children. To raise children again."

How can one ever repay such selflessness?

This is the spirit of the new world.

We think we are insignificant, but our every word and gesture and thought is fashioning and influencing the life around us moment by moment, not just the room we are in, not just the immediate vicinity, but throughout past, present and future and all of space.

Nothing is as it seems. Be as great as you can be. Fashion from your very heart the life that seems impossible.

For innumerable milennia, for countless eons, we have wandered upon this earth in a fruitless search for ourselves, for our own power, for the lost god image we had forgotten and could not remember.

For unknown kalpas, we have battled with shades and ghosts, murdering ourselves, slandering ourselves, denigrating ourselves all the while as we murdered, slandered and denigrated others.

In our blindness, we did not see ourselves.

The mirror showed us ourselves, but we slew the image in the mirror.

There has been no way out.

Now the Bomb appears, and we are forced to look within.

What is Life? Who can say?

The purpose is happiness - a happiness beyond the trite words, the trite phrases, the trite events and petty triumphs.

Happiness is a joy obtained by one who has overcome, by one who has meshed his or her own life with the gears of the vast universe without and made it their universe within. Within and without become one. This is the Buddha, the Thus Come One, who abides eternally in this world giving joy to one and all.

Opening up doors for oneself and for others, endlessly, throughout eternity, universes beyond number, universes of wonder.

Author's Works

Jim Hilgendorf's other books include "Life & Death: A Buddhist Perspective", and "The Great New Emerging Civilization". He is also the producer, along with his brother John, of the Tribute Series, a highly-acclaimed series of travel and educational videos, that are in homes, libraries and schools all across the United States, and which have appeared on PBS and international television. He is the producer of America's Dialogue, a series of national grassroots discussions about the future of America.

More information on the videos and books and America's Dialogue can be obtained at these websites:

www.tributeseries.com
www.americasdialogue.org

Printed in the United States
79742LV00002B/73-120